MEXICAN SPIRITUALISM

SPELLS & RITUALS

CARLOS ANTONIO DE BOURBON-GALDIANO-MONTENEGRO

AMERICAN CANDOMBLE CHURCH PUBLICATIONS, LOS ANGELES, CALIFORNIA

MEXICAN SPIRITUALISM

SPELLS & RITUALS

AMERICAN CANDOMBLE CHURCH PUBLICATIONS

P.O. BOX 881377

LOS ANGELES, CALIFORNIA 90009

LEGAL DISCLAIMER

No part of this book may be reproduced in any manner without written permission from the publisher or the author of this book. This book contains formulas that were used in the historical spiritual and religious practices of the Aztecs and Mexican Spiritualism. The author and the publisher do not encourage any of the practices in this book nor do we assume any liabilities for presenting those formulas or any information in this book. The formulas are presented for curious only. Neither the author, Carlos Antonio De Bourbon-Galdiano-Montenegro nor the publisher, American Candomble Church Publications assumes any responsibilities for the outcome of any of the spells, rituals or initiations in this book. We make no claims to any supernatural powers of these traditional initiation rituals. All inquiries or comments may be directed to the publisher. You must be at least 18 years of age or older to purchase this book or to purchase any of the supplies listed herein.

TABLE OF CONTENTS

LA SANTA MUERTE (The Saint of the Holy Death)

MEXICAN FOLK MAGIC

Mexican folk magic generally comes in two varieties - That of people who seek to do good and help others, and that of people who seek to do evil and harm others. The first group are generally known as *Curanderos* (or *Curanderas* if they are women), and the second group are known as *Brujas* (witches).

There is a common belief that the practices of *Curanderos* and *Curanderas* might be based primarily in the practices of Native Americans is actually a myth. Although Native American cultures have made important contributions to these arts, the fact remains that the bulk of these traditions come from Spain, where these practices survive even up to today, and that which is practiced there, and throughout the Spanish speaking world, is not that much different from what is practiced in Mexico. It was not hard, actually, during the development phase of *Curanderismo*, when Old World practices were blending with those of the New World, for them to find common ground, due to the simple fact that they had many common roots.

If you are not familiar with Mexican spiritualism, it is important to know that there are *Brujas Blanca's* (white witches) and *Brujas Negra's* (black witches). The white witches do good and the black witches cast spells for which mean or envious people pay them. Most *Mexican Witches* also practice as *Curanderas*, or practitioners of herbal medicine and home remedies.

In both types of magical practitioners, neither the *Mexican Witch* or the *Mexican Curandera* is likely to put out a sign announcing their profession as do medical doctors.

A *Curandero* or is a traditional folk healer or shaman in Latin America, who is dedicated to curing physical or spiritual illnesses. The role of a *Curandero* or *Curandera* can also incorporate the roles of psychiatrist along with that of doctor and healer. Some *Curanderos*, make use of simple herbs, waters, and even mud to affect their cures. Others additionally employ Catholic elements, such as holy water and saint pictures. The use of Roman Catholic prayers and other borrowings and lendings are often found alongside native religious elements. Beliefs vary between traditional and modern *brujos*. Traditional *brujos* hold core beliefs that are similar to or identical to the witchery around the world. Modern *brujos* are diverse and can resemble faith healers, be shamanic, spiritualists, or pagan. Practices are greatly diverse and are dependent upon the locale and the form of *brujería (witchcraft)*. Ancient forms tend to reflect the religions of the indigenous cultures, while the modern forms tend to be syncretic and use the current dominant religion (usually Catholic). The most well-known practices are similar to English witchcraft: spells (*hechizos*), charms, amulets, divination, and use of plants (usually herbs).

Among certain Hispanic and Native American cultures of the Southwest, the practice of *brujería* is feared as a manifestation of evil. Those who use rituals, spells, incantations, potions, and powders to work ill against others are known as *brujas* (witches), who are primarily female in number (the male witch is known as a *brujo*). All the negative facets of witchcraft feared by people throughout the world are practiced by the *brujas* such as manifesting the evil eye, casting spells to cause physical or mental illness, bringing about bad luck, even death. The *brujas* create dolls in which they insert bits of the victim's hair, fingernail clippings, or pieces of clothing and focus their evil intent upon the miniature representative of the person to be cursed. If a professional doctor with modern medical techniques cannot cure someone who has fallen suddenly ill, a *bruja* is suspected as being the cause of the problem.

Brujas are also thought to be accomplished shapeshifters, possessing the supernatural ability to transform themselves into owls, coyotes, or cats. As animals, they may spy upon victims and administer a potion into their unsuspecting quarry's food or water or hide a bad luck charm on their premises. There are certain amulets or rituals that claim to offer protection from the *brujas*, but one way to rid one of their evil deeds is to employ the services of a *Curandero*.

The following book explores traditional spells and magical rituals used in the practice of Mexican Spiritualism.

THE CULT OF THE SANTA MUERTE

The Santa Muerte is a sacred figure venerated in Mexico, probably a syncretism between Mesoamerican and Catholic beliefs. The name literally translates to "*Holy Death*" or "*Saint Death*." Mexican culture since the pre-Columbian era has maintained a certain reverence towards death, which can be seen in the widespread Mexican celebration of the syncretic Day of the Dead (*Dia De Los Muertos, November 1 & 2*). Catholic elements of that celebration include the use of skeletons to remind people of their mortality.

Santa Muerte generally appears as a skeletal figure, clad in a long robe and carrying one or more objects, usually a scythe and a globe. The robe is most often white, but images of the figure vary widely from person to person and according to the rite being performed or the petition of the devotee. Until recently, the religious rites and prayers of the Cult of Santa Muerte were done privately in the home. However, for the past ten years or so, worship has become more public, especially in Mexico City. The number of believers in Santa Muerte has grown over the past ten to twenty years, to approximately two million followers and has crossed the border into Mexican American communities in the United States.

MICTLANTECUHTLI, THE AZTEC GOD OF DEATH

The precise origins of the cult of Santa Muerte are a matter of debate, but it is most likely a syncretism between Mesoamerican and Catholic beliefs. Mesoamerica had always maintained a certain reverence towards death, which manifested itself among the religious practices of ancient Mexico, including in the Aztec religion. Death became personified in Aztec and other cultures in the form of humans with half their flesh missing, symbolizing the duality of life and death. The Aztecs inherited from their ancestors the gods *Mictlantecuhtli* and *Mictecacihuatl*, the Lord and Lady of Mictlan, the realm of the dead, who died of natural causes. In order for the deceased to be accepted into Mictlan, offerings to the lord and lady were necessary. Many of the offerings given then are the same as those offered to Santa Muerte today. In European Christian tradition, many paintings used skeletons to symbolize human mortality and the illusion associated with earthly life. According to many modern day anthropologists, the worship of skeletal figures has precedent in Europe during times of epidemics. These skeletal figures would be dressed up as royalty with scepters and crowns, seated on thrones to symbolize the triumph of death. In Latin America, the skeleton was used to remind Catholics of the need for a "good death," (Muerte Santa) fully confessed of sins. Bones are also associated with certain saints, such as San Pascual Bailón in Chiapas, Mexico.

After the Spanish conquest of the Aztec Empire, the cult of death diminished but was never eradicated. There are many historical references dating to 18th century Mexico. According to one account, indigenous people tied up a skeletal figure and threatened it with lashings if it did not perform miracles or grant their wishes. Another syncretism between Pre-Columbian and Christian beliefs about death can be seen in Day of the Dead celebrations. During these celebrations, hundreds flock to cemeteries to sing and pray for friends and family who have died. Children partake in the festivities by eating chocolate or candy in the shape of skulls.

In contrast to the Day of the Dead, overt worship of Santa Muerte remained hidden until the 19th century. When it surfaced, reaction was harsh, requiring the burning of any image found. One that survived this initial persecution is a skeleton made of wood, located in Chiapas, which is believed to be a replica of the skeleton of San Pascualito, who comes to people after they die. In the late 19th century, José Guadalupe Posada created a non-religious, but similar, figure by the name of Catrina, a skeleton dressed in fancy clothing of the time.

However, the cult of Santa Muerte as it is known today has become prominent only in the 20th century. The cult of Santa Muerte is said to have surged in the 1940s in lower-class neighborhoods in Mexico City. Other sources state that the modern cult has its origins around 1965 in the state of Hidalgo. It is most prevalent in Mexico State, Guerrero, Veracruz, Tamaulipas, Campeche, Morelos, and Mexico City. Lately, it has spread to Nuevo León. Together, these regions make up most of the center and northeast of the country. However, Santa Muerte can be found throughout Mexico and now in parts of the United States. There are videos, web sites, and music composed in honor of this religious expression.

Santa Muerte is referred to by a number of other names such as *Señora de las Sombras* ("Lady of the Shadows"), **Señora Blanca** ("White Lady"), *Señora Negra* ("Black Lady"), *Niña Santa* ("Holy Girl"), and *La Flaca* ("The Skinny One"). Images of Santa Muerte are generally individualistic and personal. No two are exactly the same. Sizes vary immensely from small images held in one hand to those requiring a pickup truck to move. Some people even have the image tattooed on their bodies. The appearance of the "Black Lady", "White Lady", etc. vary, but all are dressed either in long robes or (less commonly) long dresses, covered from head to feet with only the face and hands showing. This symbolizes how people hide their true selves from the rest of the world. The robe or dress covers the skeletal figure like flesh covers the bones of the living. Both are said eventually to fall away. The most common image is Santa Muerte in a robe, with a scythe in the right hand and the globe in the left. The robed image of Santa Muerte looks a bit like that of the Virgin of Guadalupe, the patron Saint of Mexico. However, there are many variations of the robe's color, and what Santa Muerte holds in her hands. Interpretations of the robe color and carried objects can vary as well.

The two most common objects that Santa Muerte carries are a scythe and a globe. The scythe can symbolize the cutting of negative energies or influences. Also, as a harvesting tool, it can symbolize hope and prosperity. It can represent the moment of death, when a scythe is said to cut a silver thread. The scythe has a long handle, indicating that it can reach anywhere. The globe represents Death's dominion, and can be seen as a kind of a tomb to which we all return.

Having the world in her hand also symbolizes vast power. Other objects that can appear with an image of Santa Muerte include scales, an hourglass, an owl, and/or an oil lamp. The scales allude to equity, justice and impartiality, as well as divine will. An hourglass indicates the time of life on earth. It also represents the belief that death is not the end, but rather the beginning of something new, as the hourglass can be turned to start over. The hourglass denotes Santa Muerte's relationship with time as well as with the worlds above and below. It also symbolizes patience. An owl symbolizes her ability to navigate the darkness and her wisdom. The owl is also said to act as a messenger. A lamp symbolizes intelligence and spirit, to light the way through the darkness of ignorance and doubt.

Often, Santa Muerte stands near statues of Catholic images of Jesus, the Virgin of Guadalupe, St. Peter, or St. Lazarus. In the north of Mexico, Santa Muerte is venerated alongside another Mexican Folkolic Saint, Jesús Malverde, However, some warn that Santa Muerte is very jealous and that her image should not be placed next to Catholic saints or there will be consequences.

Rites dedicated to Santa Muerte are similar to Catholic rites, including processions and prayers with the aim of gaining a favor. Many believers in Santa Muerte are Catholics, who invoke the name of God, Christ and the Virgin in their petitions to Santa Muerte. Altars contain an image of Santa Muerte, generally surrounded by any or all of the following: cigarettes, flowers, fruit, incense, alcoholic beverages, coins, candies and candles. According to popular belief, Santa Muerte is very powerful and is reputed to grant many favors. These images, like those of saints, are treated as real persons who can give favors in return for the faith of the believer, with miracles playing a vital role. In many ways, Santa Muerte acts like any other saint. However, Santa Muerte can grant favors that no other saint can, such as cause a person to fall in love with you, damage property, or even harm or cause the death of someone, but only in the name of justice. In exchange, the petitioner must be in the right and continue to live so. As *Señora de la Noche* ("Lady of the Night"), she is often invoked by those exposed to the dangers of working at night, such as taxi drivers, mariachi players, bar owners, police, soldiers, and prostitutes. As such, she can protect against assaults, accidents, gun violence and all types of violent death.

The image is dressed differently depending on what is being requested. Usually, the vestments of the image are differently colored robes, but it is not unknown for the image to be dressed as a bride (for those seeking a husband) or even in a colonial-era nun's habit. Associations between colors and petitions vary. White is the most common color and can symbolize loyalty, purity or the cleansing of negative influences. Red garb is for love and passion with partner and/or family. It can also signal emotional stability. Gold-colored robes indicate economic power, success, money and prosperity. Green garb signals justice or unity with loved ones. Amber or dark yellow indicates health or money. Images with this color can be seen in rehabilitation centers, especially those for drug addiction and alcoholism. In black garb, the image represents total protection against black magic or sorcery, or conversely for negative magic or for force or power. Blue garb indicates wisdom, which is favored by students and those in education. It can also be used to indicate health. Brown robes are used to invoke spirits from beyond and purple robes indicate the need to open some kind of pathway. There is also a version of the image in a rainbow-colored robe. This is called the Santa Muerte of the Seven Powers. The colors of this robe are gold, silver, copper, blue, purple, red and green. Gold is for wealth, red for love and passion, purple for the changing of negative to positive, silver for luck and success, green for justice, copper for lifting negative spirits, and blue for spirituality. In addition to the vestments, each adorns his or her own image in his or her own way, using U.S. dollars, gold coins, jewelry and other items.

Since veneration of this image has been, and to a large extent still is, private, most rituals are done in altars constructed at the homes of devotees. However, slowly, more shrines to this image are appearing in public.

As of 2009, devotion to Santa Muerte has been on the rise in the United States for the past ten years or so, mostly following the millions of Mexicans who have immigrated to the country. Evidence of devotion to her can be seen anywhere there is a large Mexican community, such as New York City, Houston, Tucson and Los Angeles.

Santo Niño de las Suertes

Niño de las Suertes

The Niño de las Suertes" is a Child Jesus image that has a strong following due to its association with Santa Muerte. While the image was created in the 19th century, its popular veneration is a recent phenomenon. The image was found by two evangelists in the rubble of the Hacienda of San Juan de Dios in Tlalpan. It was handed over to Archbishop Francisco Lizana y Beaumont. As a number of monasteries wanted to claim it, the archbishop decided to make the decision by lottery. It is said that this image favored the Convent of San Bernardo due to the vow of poverty by its nuns. This was confirmed by doing the drawing three times. In the 19th century, due to tensions between the Mexican government and the Church, the image was moved to Tacubaya when the convent was secularized. This image has a skull above the head. This originally symbolized the future Passion, has since made it associated with Santa Muerte and its devotees visit this image as well.

A Blue Statue of La Santa Muerte

Prayers and magical rituals to the Blue Santa Muerte are usually for career advancement and job success.

A Gold Statue of La Santa Muerte

Prayers and magical rituals to the Gold Santa Muerte are usually for attractions of money, business success and wealth.

A Yellow Statue of La Santa Muerte

Prayers and magical rituals to the Yellow Santa Muerte are usually to help solve any minor problems very fast.

A Transparent Amber colored Statue of La Santa Muerte

Prayers and magical rituals to the Transparent Amber Santa Muerte are usually to help people with problems of drug addiction or alcoholism.

A Green Statue of La Santa Muerte

Prayers and magical rituals to the Green Santa Muerte are usually for all matters relating to law and justice.

A Brown Statue of La Santa Muerte

Prayers and magical rituals to the Brown Santa Muerte are usually for overcoming difficult problems that we may be facing in our life.

A Black Statue of La Santa Muerte

Prayers and magical rituals to the Black Santa Muerte are usually for hexing and all works of black magic.

A Purple Statue of La Santa Muerte

Prayers and magical rituals to the Purple Santa Muerte are usually for spiritual growth and awakening psychic powers within an individual.

A Red Statue of La Santa Muerte

Prayers and magical rituals to the Red Santa Muerte are usually for domination of romance, love and attraction rituals.

A Bone colored Statue of La Santa Muerte

Prayers and magical rituals to the Bone colored Santa Muerte are usually for curing diseases of the body and helps in healing broken bones.

A Seven colored Statue of La Santa Muerte

Prayers and magical rituals to the Seven colored Santa Muerte are usually for attractions of money, business success and wealth.

A White Statue of La Santa Muerte

Prayers and magical rituals to the White Santa Muerte are usually for protection and any type of white magic spell.

HOW TO SET UP AN ALTAR FOR LA SANTA MUERTE

If you would like to set up an altar to worship the sacred mysteries of La Santa Muerte you can do the following steps;

Prepare a regular wood table that will be dedicated just for La Santa Muerte by covering it with a white, red or black cloth.

After the altar has been prepare, place the statue of La Santa Muerte in the center.

Set a white candle, a black candle and a red candle on the altar directly in front of the statue of La Santa Muerte.

Place red roses on the altar in a vase.

Place burning incense that is common for ritual ceremonies for La Santa Muerte on the altar next to her statue.

Before beginning the ritual consecration of the spiritual altar of La Santa Muerte light all of the candles.

Stand directly in front of or sit directly in front of the statue and recite the following prayer 9 times for 9 consecutive Fridays.

A GENERAL PRAYER TO LA SANTA MUERTE

Lord, before Your Divine Presence God Almighty,

Father, Son and Holy Spirit,

I ask for your permission to invoke the Holy Death.

My White daughter.

I want to humbly ask, that you break and destroy all spells and darkness that may present itself before my persona, in my home, and on my path.

Holy Death, please relieve me of all envy, poverty, hate, and unemployment and I ask that you please grant me________________.

Enlighten, with your holy presence, my home, my work and those of my loved ones, award us love, prosperity, health and wellbeing, blessed and praised by your charity Holy Death.

Lord, I give you infinite thanks, because I see your charity through your tests, which are perfecting my spirit. Lord I give you thanks, because in the midst of these tests, I will have you Holy Blessing.

Amen...

SACRED INCENSES

All of the following incenses are used by practitioners of traditional Mexican Spiritualism. Below you will find all of their magical meanings and ritual usages.

Musk Incense

This ritual incense is used to banish away negative vibrations and to remove the spirit of sickness from an individual's home.

Copal Incense

This ritual incense is used by business owners to bring new customers into their businesses.

Mirra Incense

This ritual incense is used by Mexican Spiritualists to banish away envious people and individuals who have hatred towards you.

Rose Scented Incense

This ritual incense is used to attract romance and inspire love, lust and passion.

Jasmine Scented Incense

This ritual incense is used by business owners to increase business sales and to attract new customers.

Sandalwood Incense

This ritual incense is used to bring abundance of wealth to individuals and econonmic properity new customers into their businesses.

Lilac, Vanilla, and Carnation Incense

This ritual incense is used in all matters of love, passion and seduction spells.

NOVENA PRAYER OF THE SANTA MUERTE (THE HOLY DEATH)

The following religious prayer is dedicated to the Holy Divine Mysteries of the Santa Muerte (Holy Death). The prayer is said by individuals for any special request.

In the Roman Catholic tradition, a novena is a series of prayers which are said over the course of nine days. The goal of going through a novena is to ask for grace, and to deepen one's spiritual connection with God. Although the practice of the novena originated in the Catholic community, similar prayers are also said in other Christian sects.

A novena may be said for oneself, usually as a request for assistance of some form or another, or on behalf of someone else. A classic example of a novena is a prayer asking for a sick relative to be healed. In devout communities, people may say novenas for strangers, or say "I'll make a novena for you" upon hearing of someone else's troubles.

The word "novena" comes from the Latin word for "nine." The number nine has classically been associated with sorrow in the Christian Church, and the first novena is believed to have been said by the Virgin Mary on behalf of her Son while He suffered on the cross. Several Middle Eastern and Mediterranean cultures also associated symbolic meaning with the number nine and with making prayers in sets of nine, and this tradition may have been incorporated into the Christian faith by converts who clung to old beliefs.

FIRST DAY OF THE NOVENA PRAYER

In the name of the Father, the Son and the Holy Spirit. Amen

Our Father, who art in Heaven, hallowed be thy name; thy kingdom come; thy will be done on earth as it is in heaven. Give us this day our daily bread; and forgive us our trespasses as we forgive those who trespass against us; and lead us not into temptation, but deliver us from evil. For the kingdom, the power, and the glory are yours now and forever. Amen.

Oh! Most Holy and Divine Santa Muerte: The favors that you have to grant me Will make me overcome any difficulties and help me see nothing as impossible. Not treacherous obstacles, and not one enemy. Nor let one person harm me, Let only friends come in my path, And let my businesses, and everything I do, flourish. Fill my house with riches And protect them with your virtues.

Our Father, who art in Heaven, hallowed be thy name; thy kingdom come; thy will be done on earth as it is in heaven. Give us this day our daily bread; and forgive us our trespasses as we forgive those who trespass against us; and lead us not into temptation, but deliver us from evil. For the kingdom, the power, and the glory are yours now and forever. Amen.

Our Father, who art in Heaven, hallowed be thy name; thy kingdom come; thy will be done on earth as it is in heaven. Give us this day our daily bread; and forgive us our trespasses as we forgive those who trespass against us; and lead us not into temptation, but deliver us from evil. For the

kingdom, the power, and the glory are yours now and forever. Amen.

Our Father, who art in Heaven, hallowed be thy name; thy kingdom come; thy will be done on earth as it is in heaven. Give us this day our daily bread; and forgive us our trespasses as we forgive those who trespass against us; and lead us not into temptation, but deliver us from evil. For the kingdom, the power, and the glory are yours now and forever. Amen.

Glory be to the Father and to the Son and to the Holy Spirit, as it was in the beginning, is now and ever shall be, world without end. Amen.

SECOND DAY OF THE NOVENA PRAYER

This prayer is used in Mexican Magic Love Spells

In the name of the Father, the Son and the Holy Spirit. Amen

Our Father, who art in Heaven, hallowed be thy name; thy kingdom come; thy will be done on earth as it is in heaven. Give us this day our daily bread; and forgive us our trespasses as we forgive those who trespass against us; and lead us not into temptation, but deliver us from evil. For the kingdom, the power, and the glory are yours now and forever. Amen.

Oh! Most Holy and Divine Santa Muerte, my great treasure, Never leave my side: You ate your bread and gave me a piece And as a powerful host Of the shadows in this mansion of life And empress of the darkness,

I want you to grant me this favor, that (.......)

Humbly presents themselves before my feet

Remorseful and that he never again

leave my side, so long as I need him.

Let them be able to fulfill what they promised.

Our Father, who art in Heaven, hallowed be thy name; thy kingdom come; thy will be done on earth as it is in heaven. Give us this day our daily bread; and forgive us our trespasses as we forgive those who trespass against us; and lead us not into temptation, but deliver us from evil. For the

kingdom, the power, and the glory are yours now and forever. Amen.

Our Father, who art in Heaven, hallowed be thy name; thy kingdom come; thy will be done on earth as it is in heaven. Give us this day our daily bread; and forgive us our trespasses as we forgive those who trespass against us; and lead us not into temptation, but deliver us from evil. For the kingdom, the power, and the glory are yours now and forever. Amen.

Our Father, who art in Heaven, hallowed be thy name; thy kingdom come; thy will be done on earth as it is in heaven. Give us this day our daily bread; and forgive us our trespasses as we forgive those who trespass against us; and lead us not into temptation, but deliver us from evil. For the kingdom, the power, and the glory are yours now and forever. Amen.

Glory be to the Father and to the Son and to the Holy Spirit, as it was in the beginning, is now and ever shall be, world without end. Amen.

THIRD DAY OF THE NOVENA PRAYER

In the name of the Father, the Son and the Holy Spirit. Amen

Our Father, who art in Heaven, hallowed be thy name; thy kingdom come; thy will be done on earth as it is in heaven. Give us this day our daily bread; and forgive us our trespasses as we forgive those who trespass against us; and lead us not into temptation, but deliver us from evil. For the kingdom, the power, and the glory are yours now and forever. Amen.

Oh! Most Holy and Divine Santa Muerte: Jesus, our savior, on the cross you were defeated,

let (.......) surrender at my feet.

In the name of our Lord, if they be a wild animal, they shall become tame as sheep, as soft as Rosemary flowers,

Oh! Most Holy and Divine Santa Muerte: I earnestly beg, for the massive force that God gave you to let me into (.......)'s heart...

Let (.......) have eyes only for me

And let me be everything for him/her,

Please grant me the favor that I am asking for with this Novena

And I will light a candle every Tuesday of every week at midnight in your honor

Our Father, who art in Heaven, hallowed be thy name; thy kingdom come; thy will be done on earth as it is in heaven.

Give us this day our daily bread; and forgive us our trespasses as we forgive those who trespass against us; and lead us not into temptation, but deliver us from evil. For the kingdom, the power, and the glory are yours now and forever. Amen.

Our Father, who art in Heaven, hallowed be thy name; thy kingdom come; thy will be done on earth as it is in heaven. Give us this day our daily bread; and forgive us our trespasses as we forgive those who trespass against us; and lead us not into temptation, but deliver us from evil. For the kingdom, the power, and the glory are yours now and forever. Amen.

Our Father, who art in Heaven, hallowed be thy name; thy kingdom come; thy will be done on earth as it is in heaven. Give us this day our daily bread; and forgive us our trespasses as we forgive those who trespass against us; and lead us not into temptation, but deliver us from evil. For the kingdom, the power, and the glory are yours now and forever. Amen.

Glory be to the Father and to the Son and to the Holy Spirit, as it was in the beginning, is now and ever shall be, world without end. Amen.

FOURTH DAY OF THE NOVENA PRAYER

In the name of the Father, the Son and the Holy Spirit. Amen

Our Father, who art in Heaven, hallowed be thy name; thy kingdom come; thy will be done on earth as it is in heaven. Give us this day our daily bread; and forgive us our trespasses as we forgive those who trespass against us; and lead us not into temptation, but deliver us from evil. For the kingdom, the power, and the glory are yours now and forever. Amen.

Oh! Most Holy and Divine Santa Muerte: I ask of you with all my heart, just as God made you immortal and the powerful host, queen of the never-ending shadows and that with the incredible power you possess over all that is mortal,

let (.......)

not have a table to eat,

nor a chair to sit in,

nor one moment of peace,

I want you to make him/her

come to my feet, humble and remorseful,

Draw (.......)closer and never let him/her leave again

Our Father, who art in Heaven, hallowed be thy name; thy kingdom come; thy will be done on earth as it is in heaven. Give us this day our daily bread; and forgive us our trespasses as we forgive those who trespass against us; and lead us not into temptation, but deliver us from evil. For the kingdom, the power, and the glory are yours now and forever. Amen.

Our Father, who art in Heaven, hallowed be thy name; thy kingdom come; thy will be done on earth as it is in heaven. Give us this day our daily bread; and forgive us our trespasses as we forgive those who trespass against us; and lead us not into temptation, but deliver us from evil. For the kingdom, the power, and the glory are yours now and forever. Amen.

Our Father, who art in Heaven, hallowed be thy name; thy kingdom come; thy will be done on earth as it is in heaven. Give us this day our daily bread; and forgive us our trespasses as we forgive those who trespass against us; and lead us not into temptation, but deliver us from evil. For the kingdom, the power, and the glory are yours now and forever. Amen.

Glory be to the Father and to the Son and to the Holy Spirit, as it was in the beginning, is now and ever shall be, world without end. Amen.

FIFTH DAY OF THE NOVENA PRAYER

In the name of the Father, the Son and the Holy Spirit. Amen

Our Father, who art in Heaven, hallowed be thy name; thy kingdom come; thy will be done on earth as it is in heaven. Give us this day our daily bread; and forgive us our trespasses as we forgive those who trespass against us; and lead us not into temptation, but deliver us from evil. For the kingdom, the power, and the glory are yours now and forever. Amen.

Oh! Most Holy and Divine Santa Muerte: Glorious and Powerful Death, I want to use your kindness, As my protector and host, I ask that you grant me this: Like the invincible force you are,

I beg that you make (.......)

That he/she may not find joy in his/he path,

Nor find a partner,

Nor eat, or sleep if he/she not be by my side,

Let his/her thoughts and motivation be of me and only me

Let his/her love fill me with happiness.

Our Father, who art in Heaven, hallowed be thy name; thy kingdom come; thy will be done on earth as it is in heaven. Give us this day our daily bread; and forgive us our trespasses as we forgive those who trespass against us; and lead us not into temptation, but deliver us from evil. For the

kingdom, the power, and the glory are yours now and forever. Amen.

Our Father, who art in Heaven, hallowed be thy name; thy kingdom come; thy will be done on earth as it is in heaven. Give us this day our daily bread; and forgive us our trespasses as we forgive those who trespass against us; and lead us not into temptation, but deliver us from evil. For the kingdom, the power, and the glory are yours now and forever. Amen.

Our Father, who art in Heaven, hallowed be thy name; thy kingdom come; thy will be done on earth as it is in heaven. Give us this day our daily bread; and forgive us our trespasses as we forgive those who trespass against us; and lead us not into temptation, but deliver us from evil. For the kingdom, the power, and the glory are yours now and forever. Amen.

Glory be to the Father and to the Son and to the Holy Spirit, as it was in the beginning, is now and ever shall be, world without end. Amen.

SIXTH DAY OF THE NOVENA PRAYER

In the name of the Father, the Son and the Holy Spirit. Amen

Our Father, who art in Heaven, hallowed be thy name; thy kingdom come; thy will be done on earth as it is in heaven. Give us this day our daily bread; and forgive us our trespasses as we forgive those who trespass against us; and lead us not into temptation, but deliver us from evil. For the kingdom, the power, and the glory are yours now and forever. Amen.

Oh! Most Holy and Divine Santa Muerte: Oh sovereign Lady! Whom, our Eternal Father's divine trinity elected to blind the life of the mortals, who every mortal will see, sooner or later with no regards to age or riches, as she takes old, young and new mortals whom she must take to her domain when God indicates her to. I beg that you... Let whomever fall in love with me,

Let them focus on my inner soul And not my physical beauty, Let them come to me docile, faithful and kneeling at my feet.

Our Father, who art in Heaven, hallowed be thy name; thy kingdom come; thy will be done on earth as it is in heaven. Give us this day our daily bread; and forgive us our trespasses as we forgive those who trespass against us; and lead us not into temptation, but deliver us from evil. For the kingdom, the power, and the glory are yours now and forever. Amen.

Our Father, who art in Heaven, hallowed be thy name; thy kingdom come; thy will be done on earth as it is in heaven. Give us this day our daily bread; and forgive us our trespasses as we forgive those who trespass against us; and lead us not into temptation, but deliver us from evil. For the kingdom, the power, and the glory are yours now and forever. Amen.

Our Father, who art in Heaven, hallowed be thy name; thy kingdom come; thy will be done on earth as it is in heaven. Give us this day our daily bread; and forgive us our trespasses as we forgive those who trespass against us; and lead us not into temptation, but deliver us from evil. For the kingdom, the power, and the glory are yours now and forever. Amen.

Glory be to the Father and to the Son and to the Holy Spirit, as it was in the beginning, is now and ever shall be, world without end. Amen.

SEVENTH DAY OF THE NOVENA PRAYER

In the name of the Father, the Son and the Holy Spirit. Amen

Our Father, who art in Heaven, hallowed be thy name; thy kingdom come; thy will be done on earth as it is in heaven. Give us this day our daily bread; and forgive us our trespasses as we forgive those who trespass against us; and lead us not into temptation, but deliver us from evil. For the kingdom, the power, and the glory are yours now and forever. Amen.

Oh! Most Holy and Divine Santa Muerte: Free me from all evil and with the glorious power that you possess, which God granted you, let us rejoice eternally of one glorious day without a night. This is why, my protector and master: I ask that you concede All the favors That I ask for in this Novena.

Our Father, who art in Heaven, hallowed be thy name; thy kingdom come; thy will be done on earth as it is in heaven. Give us this day our daily bread; and forgive us our trespasses as we forgive those who trespass against us; and lead us not into temptation, but deliver us from evil. For the kingdom, the power, and the glory are yours now and forever. Amen.

Our Father, who art in Heaven, hallowed be thy name; thy kingdom come; thy will be done on earth as it is in heaven. Give us this day our daily bread; and forgive us our trespasses as we forgive those who trespass against us; and lead us not into temptation, but deliver us from evil. For the kingdom, the power, and the glory are yours now and forever. Amen.

Our Father, who art in Heaven, hallowed be thy name; thy kingdom come; thy will be done on earth as it is in heaven. Give us this day our daily bread; and forgive us our trespasses as we forgive those who trespass against us; and lead us not into temptation, but deliver us from evil. For the kingdom, the power, and the glory are yours now and forever. Amen.

Glory be to the Father and to the Son and to the Holy Spirit, as it was in the beginning, is now and ever shall be, world without end. Amen.

EIGHTH DAY OF THE NOVENA PRAYER

In the name of the Father, the Son and the Holy Spirit. Amen

Our Father, who art in Heaven, hallowed be thy name; thy kingdom come; thy will be done on earth as it is in heaven. Give us this day our daily bread; and forgive us our trespasses as we forgive those who trespass against us; and lead us not into temptation, but deliver us from evil. For the kingdom, the power, and the glory are yours now and forever. Amen.

Oh! Most Holy and Divine Santa Muerte: Miraculous and Majestic Death: I ask that with your immense power,

you give back the tenderness of (.......)

Do not give him/her one moment of serenity,

nor of peace if he/she is with someone else,

nor with friends or other men/women will he/she be happy,

if asleep then let him/her dream of me,

if awake then let him/her be thinking of me

and these words I say, let him/she hear them

and grant me what I ask.

Our Father, who art in Heaven, hallowed be thy name; thy kingdom come; thy will be done on earth as it is in heaven. Give us this day our daily bread; and forgive us our trespasses as we forgive those who trespass against us; and lead us not into temptation, but deliver us from evil. For the kingdom, the power, and the glory are yours now and forever. Amen.

Our Father, who art in Heaven, hallowed be thy name; thy kingdom come; thy will be done on earth as it is in heaven. Give us this day our daily bread; and forgive us our trespasses as we forgive those who trespass against us; and lead us not into temptation, but deliver us from evil. For the kingdom, the power, and the glory are yours now and forever. Amen.

Our Father, who art in Heaven, hallowed be thy name; thy kingdom come; thy will be done on earth as it is in heaven. Give us this day our daily bread; and forgive us our trespasses as we forgive those who trespass against us; and lead us not into temptation, but deliver us from evil. For the kingdom, the power, and the glory are yours now and forever. Amen.

Glory be to the Father and to the Son and to the Holy Spirit, as it was in the beginning, is now and ever shall be, world without end. Amen.

NINTH DAY OF THE NOVENA PRAYER

In the name of the Father, the Son and the Holy Spirit. Amen

Our Father, who art in Heaven, hallowed be thy name; thy kingdom come; thy will be done on earth as it is in heaven. Give us this day our daily bread; and forgive us our trespasses as we forgive those who trespass against us; and lead us not into temptation, but deliver us from evil. For the kingdom, the power, and the glory are yours now and forever. Amen.

Oh! Most Holy and Divine Santa Muerte: Holy and Protecting Death: With the virtue that God granted you, I want you to free me of All malevolent and dangerous illness, And instead grant me: Luck, Health, Happiness, and Money, Let only friends come to me, and free me of enemies,

Making (.......)

Present himself/herself humble at my feet,

asking for forgiveness,

Humble like a lamb, and true to his/her word,

Always loving and docile.

Our Father, who art in Heaven, hallowed be thy name; thy kingdom come; thy will be done on earth as it is in heaven. Give us this day our daily bread; and forgive us our trespasses as we forgive those who trespass against us; and lead us not into temptation, but deliver us from evil. For the

kingdom, the power, and the glory are yours now and forever. Amen.

Our Father, who art in Heaven, hallowed be thy name; thy kingdom come; thy will be done on earth as it is in heaven. Give us this day our daily bread; and forgive us our trespasses as we forgive those who trespass against us; and lead us not into temptation, but deliver us from evil. For the kingdom, the power, and the glory are yours now and forever. Amen.

Our Father, who art in Heaven, hallowed be thy name; thy kingdom come; thy will be done on earth as it is in heaven. Give us this day our daily bread; and forgive us our trespasses as we forgive those who trespass against us; and lead us not into temptation, but deliver us from evil. For the kingdom, the power, and the glory are yours now and forever. Amen.

Glory be to the Father and to the Son and to the Holy Spirit, as it was in the beginning, is now and ever shall be, world without end. Amen.

NINO FIDENCIO CONSTANTINO

THE HISTORY OF NINO FIDENCIO CONSTANTINO

El Niño Fidencio (born 1898; died Espinazo, Mina, Nuevo León, October 19, 1938) was a famous Mexican Curandero. His birth name was José de Jesús Fidencio Constantino Síntora. Today he is revered by the Fidencista Christian Church. The Catholic Church does not recognize his official status as a saint, but his following has extended through the northern part of Mexico and the southwest of United States. This situation allows El Niño Fidencio to be recognized as a folk saint.

While in elementary school, he met Father Segura, as well as Enrique López de la Fuente, who was the janitor as well as his friend, and later, his protector. They both worked to help the priest with religious services, and it was at this time that Fidencio learned to work with herbs and how to cure.

In 1912, Enrique and Fidencio left for the City of Morelia, Michoacán, where the latter worked until he decided to join the Mexican Revolution, causing them to be separated for nine years. Fidencio then moved to Loma Sola, Coahuila, where he lived with his sister Antonia.

At the age of fifteen, Fidencio attended school in Mina, Nuevo León, a town close to Espinazo. According to Raúl Cadena, Fidencio did not develop sexually, was always clean-shaven, had a soft voice, and never engaged in sexual activity.

In 1921, Enrique returned from the revolutionary struggle and went to work for Antonio L. Rodríguez at the San Rafael mine in Espinazo. There he had several children, and, needing help in caring for them, went to his childhood friend.

Fidencio came to town that year, and remained there for the rest of his life. It was at this point that he began to perform healings.

On February 8, 1928, President Plutarco Elías Calles visited Espinazo and attended a healing session with Niño Fidencio. Although the president's ailment was unknown to the public at the time, Enrique records that he was suffering from nodular leprosy.

Fidencio was famous for performing operations without anaesthesia without causing pain to patients, and provided cures related to specific parts of town, such as a pepper tree which the congregation threw offerings around, and a mud puddle in which his followers bathed.

According to devotees, Fidencio continues to work miracles through objects called Little Boxes.

During his life, a multitude of imitators and impostors appeared, the death of one of whom was mistaken for Fidencio's own. The falsified death was announced by the press, and his funeral prompted a massive outpouring of emotion. His actual death came just over a year later. Decades later, he is still well known in the town of Espinazo, and plays a significant part in the town's economy by generating tourism and the sale of religious objects and services.

Fidencio's first attempt at healing was the spontaneous act of setting his mother's arm, broken in a fall. Although the splinting of an arm hardly seems remarkable, Fidencio was said to be eight years old at the time.

At Espinazo, Fidencio developed a considerable reputation for treating animals, especially assisting at births. But it was not until he was called upon to assist with a human birth that his ability and fame as a healer and midwife began to unfold.

During the course of his lifetime, El Niño Fidencio had several supernatural experiences in the form of revelations or visions--some, he claimed, were visitations by Jesus Christ.

In an early vision, Fidencio was visited by a strange, bearded man who imbued him with the spiritual gift of healing, which included profound knowledge of medicinal plants. Although Fidencio never had any formal training in the healing properties of plants and home remedies, he was expert in their use.

A second supernatural visitation occurred in 1927. This mystical event played a significant role in Fidencio's life. He felt it authorized him to share his gift of healing with the masses of needy and, thus, begin his mission on Earth. From this time on, Fidencio adopted the persona of a holy man and lived the life of an ascetic. He achieved fame as a healer in 1928, at the age of 30. He died ten years later, a few days short of his fortieth birthday. Even in death his miracles are still very much real. You can pray to him for any need you may have.

FIDENCIO S. CONSTANTINO
(EL NIÑO GUADALUPANO)

A PRAYER TO NINO FIDENCIO CONSTANTINO

A powerful devotional prayer Novena to Nino Fidencio Constantino. This Novena prayer should be recited daily for nine consecutive days. This power prayer is for any special spiritual request.

NOVENA PRAYER

In the name of the Father, the Son and the Holy Spirit. Amen

Our Father, who art in Heaven, hallowed be thy name; thy kingdom come; thy will be done on earth as it is in heaven. Give us this day our daily bread; and forgive us our trespasses as we forgive those who trespass against us; and lead us not into temptation, but deliver us from evil. For the kingdom, the power, and the glory are yours now and forever. Amen.

Hail Mary, full of grace. Our Lord is with thee. Blessed art thou among women, and blessed is the fruit of thy womb, Jesus. Holy Mary, Mother of God, pray for us sinners, now and at the hour of our death. Amen.

O Most Holy and Divine Servant of God, Nino Fidencio Constantino be my light and guidance from your heavenly home. I call upon you in my time of need.

Full of faith in the miracles, you have bestowed upon those in the living

(make your petition)

In confidence await you answer. In return for granting me what I ask I promise to spread your name To those who are unaware of your kindness.

Glory be to the Father and to the Son and to the Holy Spirit, as it was in the beginning, is now and ever shall be, world without end. Amen.

JESUS MALVERDE

THE HISTORY OF JESUS MALVERDE

Jesús Malverde, sometimes known as the "generous bandit", "angel of the poor", is a folklore hero in the Mexican state of Sinaloa. He is celebrated as a folk saint by some in Mexico and the United States. He is not recognized as a saint by the Roman Catholic Church.

NOVENA PRAYER OF JESUS MALVERDE

FIRST DAY OF THE NOVENA

In the name of the Father, the Son and the Holy Spirit. Amen

Our Father, who art in Heaven, hallowed be thy name; thy kingdom come; thy will be done on earth as it is in heaven. Give us this day our daily bread; and forgive us our trespasses as we forgive those who trespass against us; and lead us not into temptation, but deliver us from evil. For the kingdom, the power, and the glory are yours now and forever. Amen.

Oh Most Glorious Jesus Malverde, today I humbly kneel at the foot of the most Holy Cross.

Oh Most Glorious Jesus Malverde, today I ask you to alleviate my misery and my suffering.

Oh Most Glorious Jesus Malverde, you are most favorite of God and I ask you to intercede on my behalf.

Oh Most Glorious Jesus Malverde, hear my prayer request.

Oh Most Glorious Jesus Malverde, Saint of the Impossible, hear my prayer.

Oh Most Glorious Jesus Malverde, Most humble servant of God, hear my prayer request.

Oh Most Glorious Jesus Malverde, grant me peace.

Oh Most Glorious Jesus Malverde, grant me good health.

Oh Most Glorious Jesus Malverde, grant me abundance of wealth.

Oh Most Glorious Jesus Malverde protect me from all enemies known and unknown.

Oh Most Glorious Jesus Malverde, just as the deer jumps over all obstacles in its path so may you give me the ability to leap over any and all obstacles and enemies in my path.

Oh Most Glorious Jesus Malverde, I pray that you hear my prayers today. Amen

Glory be to the Father and to the Son and to the Holy Spirit, as it was in the beginning, is now and ever shall be, world without end. Amen.

-State Your Prayer Request-

SECOND DAY OF THE NOVENA

In the name of the Father, the Son and the Holy Spirit. Amen

Our Father, who art in Heaven, hallowed be thy name; thy kingdom come; thy will be done on earth as it is in heaven. Give us this day our daily bread; and forgive us our trespasses as we forgive those who trespass against us; and lead us not into temptation, but deliver us from evil. For the kingdom, the power, and the glory are yours now and forever. Amen.

Oh Most Glorious Jesus Malverde, today I humbly kneel at the foot of the most Holy Cross.

Oh Most Glorious Jesus Malverde, today I ask you to alleviate my misery and my suffering.

Oh Most Glorious Jesus Malverde, you are most favorite of God and I ask you to intercede on my behalf.

Oh Most Glorious Jesus Malverde, hear my prayer request.

Oh Most Glorious Jesus Malverde, Saint of the Impossible, hear my prayer.

Oh Most Glorious Jesus Malverde, Most humble servant of God, hear my prayer request.

Oh Most Glorious Jesus Malverde, grant me peace.

Oh Most Glorious Jesus Malverde, grant me good health.

Oh Most Glorious Jesus Malverde, grant me abundance of wealth.

Oh Most Glorious Jesus Malverde protect me from all enemies known and unknown.

Oh Most Glorious Jesus Malverde, just as the deer jumps over all obstacles in its path so may you give me the ability to leap over any and all obstacles and enemies in my path.

Oh Most Glorious Jesus Malverde, I pray that you hear my prayers today. Amen

Glory be to the Father and to the Son and to the Holy Spirit, as it was in the beginning, is now and ever shall be, world without end. Amen.

-State Your Prayer Request-

THIRD DAY OF THE NOVENA

In the name of the Father, the Son and the Holy Spirit. Amen

Our Father, who art in Heaven, hallowed be thy name; thy kingdom come; thy will be done on earth as it is in heaven. Give us this day our daily bread; and forgive us our trespasses as we forgive those who trespass against us; and lead us not into temptation, but deliver us from evil. For the kingdom, the power, and the glory are yours now and forever. Amen.

Oh Most Glorious Jesus Malverde, today I humbly kneel at the foot of the most Holy Cross.

Oh Most Glorious Jesus Malverde, today I ask you to alleviate my misery and my suffering.

Oh Most Glorious Jesus Malverde, you are most favorite of God and I ask you to intercede on my behalf.

Oh Most Glorious Jesus Malverde, hear my prayer request.

Oh Most Glorious Jesus Malverde, Saint of the Impossible, hear my prayer.

Oh Most Glorious Jesus Malverde, Most humble servant of God, hear my prayer request.

Oh Most Glorious Jesus Malverde, grant me peace.

Oh Most Glorious Jesus Malverde, grant me good health.

Oh Most Glorious Jesus Malverde, grant me abundance of wealth.

Oh Most Glorious Jesus Malverde protect me from all enemies known and unknown.

Oh Most Glorious Jesus Malverde, just as the deer jumps over all obstacles in its path so may you give me the ability to leap over any and all obstacles and enemies in my path.

Oh Most Glorious Jesus Malverde, I pray that you hear my prayers today. Amen

Glory be to the Father and to the Son and to the Holy Spirit, as it was in the beginning, is now and ever shall be, world without end. Amen.

-State Your Prayer Request-

FOURTH DAY OF THE NOVENA

In the name of the Father, the Son and the Holy Spirit. Amen

Our Father, who art in Heaven, hallowed be thy name; thy kingdom come; thy will be done on earth as it is in heaven. Give us this day our daily bread; and forgive us our trespasses as we forgive those who trespass against us; and lead us not into temptation, but deliver us from evil. For the kingdom, the power, and the glory are yours now and forever. Amen.

Oh Most Glorious Jesus Malverde, today I humbly kneel at the foot of the most Holy Cross.

Oh Most Glorious Jesus Malverde, today I ask you to alleviate my misery and my suffering.

Oh Most Glorious Jesus Malverde, you are most favorite of God and I ask you to intercede on my behalf.

Oh Most Glorious Jesus Malverde, hear my prayer request.

Oh Most Glorious Jesus Malverde, Saint of the Impossible, hear my prayer.

Oh Most Glorious Jesus Malverde, Most humble servant of God, hear my prayer request.

Oh Most Glorious Jesus Malverde, grant me peace.

Oh Most Glorious Jesus Malverde, grant me good health.

Oh Most Glorious Jesus Malverde, grant me abundance of wealth.

Oh Most Glorious Jesus Malverde protect me from all enemies known and unknown.

Oh Most Glorious Jesus Malverde, just as the deer jumps over all obstacles in its path so may you give me the ability to leap over any and all obstacles and enemies in my path.

Oh Most Glorious Jesus Malverde, I pray that you hear my prayers today. Amen

Glory be to the Father and to the Son and to the Holy Spirit, as it was in the beginning, is now and ever shall be, world without end. Amen.

-State Your Prayer Request-

FIFTH DAY OF THE NOVENA

In the name of the Father, the Son and the Holy Spirit. Amen

Our Father, who art in Heaven, hallowed be thy name; thy kingdom come; thy will be done on earth as it is in heaven. Give us this day our daily bread; and forgive us our trespasses as we forgive those who trespass against us; and lead us not into temptation, but deliver us from evil. For the kingdom, the power, and the glory are yours now and forever. Amen.

Oh Most Glorious Jesus Malverde, today I humbly kneel at the foot of the most Holy Cross.

Oh Most Glorious Jesus Malverde, today I ask you to alleviate my misery and my suffering.

Oh Most Glorious Jesus Malverde, you are most favorite of God and I ask you to intercede on my behalf.

Oh Most Glorious Jesus Malverde, hear my prayer request.

Oh Most Glorious Jesus Malverde, Saint of the Impossible, hear my prayer.

Oh Most Glorious Jesus Malverde, Most humble servant of God, hear my prayer request.

Oh Most Glorious Jesus Malverde, grant me peace.

Oh Most Glorious Jesus Malverde, grant me good health.

Oh Most Glorious Jesus Malverde, grant me abundance of wealth.

Oh Most Glorious Jesus Malverde protect me from all enemies known and unknown.

Oh Most Glorious Jesus Malverde, just as the deer jumps over all obstacles in its path so may you give me the ability to leap over any and all obstacles and enemies in my path.

Oh Most Glorious Jesus Malverde, I pray that you hear my prayers today. Amen

Glory be to the Father and to the Son and to the Holy Spirit, as it was in the beginning, is now and ever shall be, world without end. Amen.

-State Your Prayer Request-

SIXTH DAY OF THE NOVENA

In the name of the Father, the Son and the Holy Spirit. Amen

Our Father, who art in Heaven, hallowed be thy name; thy kingdom come; thy will be done on earth as it is in heaven. Give us this day our daily bread; and forgive us our trespasses as we forgive those who trespass against us; and lead us not into temptation, but deliver us from evil. For the kingdom, the power, and the glory are yours now and forever. Amen.

Oh Most Glorious Jesus Malverde, today I humbly kneel at the foot of the most Holy Cross.

Oh Most Glorious Jesus Malverde, today I ask you to alleviate my misery and my suffering.

Oh Most Glorious Jesus Malverde, you are most favorite of God and I ask you to intercede on my behalf.

Oh Most Glorious Jesus Malverde, hear my prayer request.

Oh Most Glorious Jesus Malverde, Saint of the Impossible, hear my prayer.

Oh Most Glorious Jesus Malverde, Most humble servant of God, hear my prayer request.

Oh Most Glorious Jesus Malverde, grant me peace.

Oh Most Glorious Jesus Malverde, grant me good health.

Oh Most Glorious Jesus Malverde, grant me abundance of wealth.

Oh Most Glorious Jesus Malverde protect me from all enemies known and unknown.

Oh Most Glorious Jesus Malverde, just as the deer jumps over all obstacles in its path so may you give me the ability to leap over any and all obstacles and enemies in my path.

Oh Most Glorious Jesus Malverde, I pray that you hear my prayers today. Amen

Glory be to the Father and to the Son and to the Holy Spirit, as it was in the beginning, is now and ever shall be, world without end. Amen.

-State Your Prayer Request-

SEVENTH DAY OF THE NOVENA

In the name of the Father, the Son and the Holy Spirit. Amen

Our Father, who art in Heaven, hallowed be thy name; thy kingdom come; thy will be done on earth as it is in heaven. Give us this day our daily bread; and forgive us our trespasses as we forgive those who trespass against us; and lead us not into temptation, but deliver us from evil. For the kingdom, the power, and the glory are yours now and forever. Amen.

Oh Most Glorious Jesus Malverde, today I humbly kneel at the foot of the most Holy Cross.

Oh Most Glorious Jesus Malverde, today I ask you to alleviate my misery and my suffering.

Oh Most Glorious Jesus Malverde, you are most favorite of God and I ask you to intercede on my behalf.

Oh Most Glorious Jesus Malverde, hear my prayer request.

Oh Most Glorious Jesus Malverde, Saint of the Impossible, hear my prayer.

Oh Most Glorious Jesus Malverde, Most humble servant of God, hear my prayer request.

Oh Most Glorious Jesus Malverde, grant me peace.

Oh Most Glorious Jesus Malverde, grant me good health.

Oh Most Glorious Jesus Malverde, grant me abundance of wealth.

Oh Most Glorious Jesus Malverde protect me from all enemies known and unknown.

Oh Most Glorious Jesus Malverde, just as the deer jumps over all obstacles in its path so may you give me the ability to leap over any and all obstacles and enemies in my path.

Oh Most Glorious Jesus Malverde, I pray that you hear my prayers today. Amen

Glory be to the Father and to the Son and to the Holy Spirit, as it was in the beginning, is now and ever shall be, world without end. Amen.

-State Your Prayer Request-

EIGHTH DAY OF THE NOVENA

In the name of the Father, the Son and the Holy Spirit. Amen

Our Father, who art in Heaven, hallowed be thy name; thy kingdom come; thy will be done on earth as it is in heaven. Give us this day our daily bread; and forgive us our trespasses as we forgive those who trespass against us; and lead us not into temptation, but deliver us from evil. For the kingdom, the power, and the glory are yours now and forever. Amen.

Oh Most Glorious Jesus Malverde, today I humbly kneel at the foot of the most Holy Cross.

Oh Most Glorious Jesus Malverde, today I ask you to alleviate my misery and my suffering.

Oh Most Glorious Jesus Malverde, you are most favorite of God and I ask you to intercede on my behalf.

Oh Most Glorious Jesus Malverde, hear my prayer request.

Oh Most Glorious Jesus Malverde, Saint of the Impossible, hear my prayer.

Oh Most Glorious Jesus Malverde, Most humble servant of God, hear my prayer request.

Oh Most Glorious Jesus Malverde, grant me peace.

Oh Most Glorious Jesus Malverde, grant me good health.

Oh Most Glorious Jesus Malverde, grant me abundance of wealth.

Oh Most Glorious Jesus Malverde protect me from all enemies known and unknown.

Oh Most Glorious Jesus Malverde, just as the deer jumps over all obstacles in its path so may you give me the ability to leap over any and all obstacles and enemies in my path.

Oh Most Glorious Jesus Malverde, I pray that you hear my prayers today. Amen

Glory be to the Father and to the Son and to the Holy Spirit, as it was in the beginning, is now and ever shall be, world without end. Amen.

-State Your Prayer Request-

NINTH DAY OF THE NOVENA

In the name of the Father, the Son and the Holy Spirit. Amen

Our Father, who art in Heaven, hallowed be thy name; thy kingdom come; thy will be done on earth as it is in heaven. Give us this day our daily bread; and forgive us our trespasses as we forgive those who trespass against us; and lead us not into temptation, but deliver us from evil. For the kingdom, the power, and the glory are yours now and forever. Amen.

Oh Most Glorious Jesus Malverde, today I humbly kneel at the foot of the most Holy Cross.

Oh Most Glorious Jesus Malverde, today I ask you to alleviate my misery and my suffering.

Oh Most Glorious Jesus Malverde, you are most favorite of God and I ask you to intercede on my behalf.

Oh Most Glorious Jesus Malverde, hear my prayer request.

Oh Most Glorious Jesus Malverde, Saint of the Impossible, hear my prayer.

Oh Most Glorious Jesus Malverde, Most humble servant of God, hear my prayer request.

Oh Most Glorious Jesus Malverde, grant me peace.

Oh Most Glorious Jesus Malverde, grant me good health.

Oh Most Glorious Jesus Malverde, grant me abundance of wealth.

Oh Most Glorious Jesus Malverde protect me from all enemies known and unknown.

Oh Most Glorious Jesus Malverde, just as the deer jumps over all obstacles in its path so may you give me the ability to leap over any and all obstacles and enemies in my path.

Oh Most Glorious Jesus Malverde, I pray that you hear my prayers today. Amen

Glory be to the Father and to the Son and to the Holy Spirit, as it was in the beginning, is now and ever shall be, world without end. Amen.

-State Your Prayer Request-

TO ATTRACT MONEY

Place a Gold Statue of La Santa Muerte on your spiritual altar. Dress a green pillar candle using money drawing oil. After you have dressed the candle, sprinkle gold magnetic sand over the candle so that the magnetic sand sticks to the sides of the candle with the money drawing oil. Place the candle directly in front of the image of La Santa Muerte and then light it. After you light the candle then burn Sandalwood Incense. Burn the incense in an incense burner and place it on your spiritual altar next to the image of La Santa Muerte. Recite the general prayer to La Santa Muerte. Do this ritual for seven consecutive days.

TO ATTRACT JOB SUCCESS

Place a Blue Statue of La Santa Muerte on your spiritual altar. Dress a yellow pillar candle using patchouli oil. After you have dressed the candle, sprinkle green magnetic sand over the candle so that the magnetic sand sticks to the sides of the candle with the patchouli oil. Place the candle directly in front of the image of La Santa Muerte and then light it. After you light the candle then burn Sandalwood Incense. Burn the incense in an incense burner and place it on your spiritual altar next to the image of La Santa Muerte. Recite the general prayer to La Santa Muerte. Do this ritual for three consecutive days.

TO ATTRACT CLIENTS TO A BUSINESS

Place a Seven colored Statue of La Santa Muerte on your spiritual altar. Dress a seven colored pillar candle using frankincense & myrrh oil. After you have dressed the candle, sprinkle gold magnetic sand over the candle so that the magnetic sand sticks to the sides of the candle with the frankincense & myrrh oil. Place the candle directly in front of the image of La Santa Muerte and then light it. After you light the candle then burn Copal Incense. Burn the incense in an incense burner and place it on your spiritual altar next to the image of La Santa Muerte. Recite the general prayer to La Santa Muerte. Do this ritual for seven consecutive days.

TO REMOVE WITCHCRAFT

Place a White Statue of La Santa Muerte on your spiritual altar. Dress a black & red reversible pillar candle using camphor oil. After you have dressed the candle, sprinkle silver magnetic sand over the candle so that the magnetic sand sticks to the sides of the candle with the camphor oil. Place the candle directly in front of the image of La Santa Muerte and then light it. After you light the candle then burn Musk Incense. Burn the incense in an incense burner and place it on your spiritual altar next to the image of La Santa Muerte. Recite the general prayer to La Santa Muerte. Do this ritual for nine consecutive days.

TO ATTRACT AN INDIVIDUAL TO YOU FOR ROMANCE

Place a Red Statue of La Santa Muerte on your spiritual altar. Dress a pink pillar candle using rose oil. After you have dressed the candle, sprinkle red magnetic sand over the candle so that the magnetic sand sticks to the sides of the candle with the money rose oil. Place the candle directly in front of the image of La Santa Muerte and then light it. After you light the candle then burn Lilac, Vanilla and Carnation Incense. Burn the incense in an incense burner and place it on your spiritual altar next to the image of La Santa Muerte. Recite the general prayer to La Santa Muerte. Do this ritual for five consecutive days.

TO FIND FAST EMPLOYMENT

Place a Blue Statue of La Santa Muerte on your spiritual altar. Dress an orange pillar candle using Jasmine and Orange oil. After you have dressed the candle, sprinkle gold magnetic sand over the candle so that the magnetic sand sticks to the sides of the candle with the Jasmine and Orange oil. Place the candle directly in front of the image of La Santa Muerte and then light it. After you light the candle then burn Rose scented Incense. Burn the incense in an incense burner and place it on your spiritual altar next to the image of La Santa Muerte. Recite the general prayer to La Santa Muerte. Do this ritual for three consecutive days.

TO BANISH SICKNESS

Place a Bone colored Statue of La Santa Muerte on your spiritual altar. Dress a purple pillar candle using coconut oil. After you have dressed the candle, sprinkle silver magnetic sand over the candle so that the magnetic sand sticks to the sides of the candle with the coconut oil. Place the candle directly in front of the image of La Santa Muerte and then light it. After you light the candle then burn Mirra Incense. Burn the incense in an incense burner and place it on your spiritual altar next to the image of La Santa Muerte. Recite the general prayer to La Santa Muerte. Do this ritual for nine consecutive days.

TO BANISH NEGATIVE VIBRATION

Place a Transparent Amber Statue of La Santa Muerte on your spiritual altar. Dress a silver pillar candle using dragon's blood oil. After you have dressed the candle, sprinkle silver magnetic sand over the candle so that the magnetic sand sticks to the sides of the candle with the dragon's blood oil. Place the candle directly in front of the image of La Santa Muerte and then light it. After you light the candle then burn Mirra Incense. Burn the incense in an incense burner and place it on your spiritual altar next to the image of La Santa Muerte. Recite the general prayer to La Santa Muerte. Do this ritual for seven consecutive days.

TO CAUSE CONFLICTS BETWEEN TWO INDIVIDUALS

Place a Black Statue of La Santa Muerte on your spiritual altar. Dress a black pillar candle using conflict and destructions oil. After you have dressed the candle, sprinkle conflict powder over the candle so that the conflict powder sticks to the sides of the candle with the conflict and destruction oil. Place the candle directly in front of the image of La Santa Muerte and then light it. After you light the candle then burn Mirra Incense. Burn the incense in an incense burner and place it on your spiritual altar next to the image of La Santa Muerte. Recite the general prayer to La Santa Muerte. Do this ritual for nine consecutive days.

TO BRING GAMBLING SUCCESS

Place a Seven colored Statue of La Santa Muerte on your spiritual altar. Dress a green pillar candle using bayberry oil. After you have dressed the candle, sprinkle gold magnetic sand over the candle so that the magnetic sand sticks to the sides of the candle with the bayberry oil. Place the candle directly in front of the image of La Santa Muerte and then light it. After you light the candle then burn Sandalwood Incense. Burn the incense in an incense burner and place it on your spiritual altar next to the image of La Santa Muerte. Recite the general prayer to La Santa Muerte. Do this ritual for three consecutive days.

TO MAKE A LOST LOVE RETURN TO YOU

Place a Yellow Statue of La Santa Muerte on your spiritual altar. Dress a blue pillar candle using lotus oil. After you have dressed the candle, sprinkle silver magnetic sand over the candle so that the magnetic sand sticks to the sides of the candle with the lotus oil. Place the candle directly in front of the image of La Santa Muerte and then light it. After you light the candle then burn Rose scented Incense. Burn the incense in an incense burner and place it on your spiritual altar next to the image of La Santa Muerte. Recite the general prayer to La Santa Muerte. Do this ritual for seven consecutive days.

TO MAKE AN INDIVIDUAL CALL YOU

Place a Red Statue of La Santa Muerte on your spiritual altar. Dress a pink pillar candle using cinnamon oil. After you have dressed the candle, sprinkle gold magnetic sand over the candle so that the magnetic sand sticks to the sides of the candle with the cinnamon oil. Place the candle directly in front of the image of La Santa Muerte and then light it. After you light the candle then burn Lilac, Vanilla and Carnation Incense. Burn the incense in an incense burner and place it on your spiritual altar next to the image of La Santa Muerte. Recite the general prayer to La Santa Muerte. Do this ritual for seven consecutive days.

SPIRITUAL OIL
SPIRITUAL OIL
SPIRITUAL OIL
SPIRITUAL OIL

www.ingramcontent.com/pod-product-compliance
Ingram Content Group UK Ltd.
Pitfield, Milton Keynes, MK11 3LW, UK
UKHW041924190726
13854UKWH00003B/1422